Aporia

Poems by

Eric E. Hyett

LILY POETRY REVIEW BOOKS

Published by Lily Poetry Review Books
223 Winter Street
Whitman, MA 02382

https://lilypoetryreview.blog/

ISBN: 978-1-7365990-9-9

Cover design: Martha McCollough

For my mother,

Barbara Helfgott Hyett (b. 1945)

Contents

Alzheimer's Spring

1. The Voice of the Lad / 1
2. Today / 2
3. Seder Plate / 3
4. Gefilte Fish / 4
5. Redemption is Not Yet Complete / 5
6. Wash Your Hands But Do Not Say The Blessing / 6
7. My Mom, The Moon / 7
8. And To Whom Am I Speaking? / 8
9. I'm Not Saying I'm Going To Change / 9
10. Checkboxes / 10
11. Wind-Blown Glory / 11
12. Late Spring or Early Summer, Depending / 12

Alzheimer's Summer

1. Come Thunder / 15
2. Diagonale du Vide - Empty Diagonal / 16
3. My Mother Yawns / 17
4. Perfectly Fine / 18
5. To See Clear / 19
6. My Mother, The Rain / 20
7. Teaching My Mother's Poetry Workshop / 21
8. July 19th / 22
9. Caregiver Fatigue / 23
10. My Mom Categorizes Poems / 24
11. Eye Contact / 25

Alzheimer's Fall

1. The Wind Slams Eastward Down Beacon Street / 29
2. Janice / 30
3. Razing The Tenements in Atlantic City / 31
4. On A Slippery Slope? / 32

5. Unfilled Timetables / 33

6. June, 1982/ / 34

7. Take The 'Sim' Out of Simple / 35

8. The Dance Continued 'Til Two / 36

9. History Of Gunpowder / 37

10. Because / 38

11. Thanksgiving Day Is Hailed With Joy / 39

12. Suppose We Could Do The Opposite / 40

Alzheimer's Winter

1. The Rest of The Coffee / 43

2. Painted-On Contents of the Painted-On Bookshelves / 44

3. From The Greek / 45

4. I Don't Want To See This. I Don't. / 46

5. Shiva / 47

6. The Nutcracker / 48

7. Memories of Amsterdam / 49

8. Now There's A Woman! / 50

9. Last Year / 51

Acknowledgements / 53

ALZHEIMER'S SPRING

I. The Voice of the Lad

From Mount Auburn Hospital
to Harvard Square
is a four-minute bus ride:
such a great distance to cover
in such a short time.

I receive a text message
from a friend:

You should feel the team is a village,
and we're all going to find the best
care, the best place for her.

Her meaning my mom.

I tell Wendy I don't feel part of a village.
I feel completely alone
in the village of unsolicited advice
of which I am the mayor.
Also, the village idiot.

2. Today

My mom tells me about the game she's
playing— *the game,* she calls it—

I won't accept treatment.
I won't be taken in.
I will care for myself.

I tell her it's a battle royale.
A lot of damage
can still be inflicted.

I make her hot cocoa:
I've become outstanding at styrofoam cups
and the Geriatric Psych Unit's
microwave.

3. Seder Plate

The green parsley represents me
at my criminal trial.

The roasted egg
is what happened to the dinosaurs.

The bitter herb represents
Herb, Wendy's husband.

I will not let the salt water
symbolize my tears.

The shank bone represents the spare ribs
at Golden Temple in Washington Square;
also, the sacrifices my parents made.

The red wine symbolizes
itself, repeatedly.

The hidden *Afikoman*
is my mom.

4. Gefilte Fish

On Friday, I'll go pick some up
at Elissa's apartment: Elissa
had to make gefilte fish without
my mom this year.

It's an acquired taste, gefilte fish—
the smell, the braising:
21 pounds of whitefish, pike and carp,
the extra fish heads Elissa
orders for the broth,
the espresso Elissa serves me
in a white porcelain cup.

I drink it on the balcony
as I inspect the Charles
eleven stories below:
great background for a selfie.

I call Elissa out from the kitchen
to take the photo
I'll show my mother later.

I just want her to remember
the tradition.

5. Redemption is Not Yet Complete

Maybe the world's
already perfect,

and the Messiah's
my mother

in pink pajamas
and with adequate supply

of crayons to color my
shattered world,

to pass final judgment,
to say *yep,*

this world's all set—
the messiah who

used to hand me a five-dollar
bill each time we parted

and say *here's*
fi dollahs.

6. Wash Your Hands But Do Not Say The Blessing

I bless the Purel
outside my mother's room.

Next, Elijah.
He's my Lyft,
parked outside the hospital.

On Passover, in our family,
the Cup of Miriam is set out.
I'm trying to honor the holiday
so I've named my mother's Subaru
The Cup Of Miriam
and washed it.

I could go as far
as the story of Exodus—
drive south on I-95
all the way to Palm Beach.

7. My Mom, The Moon

Our last lucid conversation
on the air
that hangs like moonlight.

A fragment of something—
our last lucid conversation
so long ago it seems

a fragment of something.
Yesterday?
So long ago it seems

but tonight's exactly
yesterday
like every night in Eden:

tonight exactly
full of promises
like every night in Eden,

full of promise, the moon:
when she's new,
she's invisible.

8. And To Whom Am I Speaking?

Three times this week, something
completely surprising happened.

My mug exploded:
gash like a fish hook
in my hand.

3:10 A.M.: woke with
the sense that I couldn't breathe,
sound of traffic like the ocean.

I had my mother's table delivered
to my house, had my table delivered
to Alexis's house.

Lately, things come in like the tide—

How are my furnishings? my mother asks,
not in the conventional sense.

9. I'm Not Saying I'm Going To Change

We are not permitted to linger,
Rilke wrote,
even with what is most intimate.

That quote was the entry
in my high school yearbook,
next to a picture of me in the crewneck
sweater my mom said to wear.

She was right, by the way, about keeping me
classy in that yearbook—
no references to weed,
not even *What a long strange*
trip it's been, which was my first choice.
My mom talked me out of
that cliché.

10. Checkboxes

☒ You may photocopy this consent form.

☒ You may bind it as a symbol before my mother's eyes.

☒ You may bless my mother when she sneezes

☒ And when she doesn't sneeze, bless the smell of urine.

☒ You have my permission to flush her down

☒ And when you do, sing *Summertime*.

Leave the moon on? Circle one. (Y / N)

11. Wind-Blown Glory

(after Vanitas *by Richard Hoffman)*

My hair, coming home after skiing.
And the time my brother and I

were those crazy people dancing on the seawall
behind the StormWatch meteorologist.

Also, the glory of my mother.
The windblown, glorious truth

of her bloodstained trenchcoat.
23 stitches. A concussion. The night

we both knew
for sure.

12. Late Spring or Early Summer, Depending

We all turn into something.
The grape becomes the raisin. The olive
becomes the topping on a salade Niçoise.

Cranberries become Craisins,
cherries turn tart, dried.
Sometimes we become a leather-bound
edition of ourselves:
a boy with pure song in his heart
becomes ancient, craggy,
or Bob Dylan.

Sometimes chocolate
turns into irony.
Something faded.

My mother's spirit
turns into
whatever she is now.   -

ALZHEIMER'S SUMMER

1. Come Thunder

When it rains
in the city
on a summer night
the pavement gives back heat
as steam—

In this version, the rain
is my mother,
and the pavement,
a long dry spell.

In another version
the pavement is my mom
and I'm the rain,
falling from the cloud
where I've been
gathering.

2. Diagonale du Vide—Empty Diagonal

I'm at the Prehistory Museum
in Les Eyzies-de-Tayac-Sireuil
when my mom's psychiatrist calls.
She asks me point blank: *How can I
make your mother less anxious?*

Paradoxically, tranquilizers
have the opposite effect.

That night, I try calling my mom.
Really? she says.
*Wait a minute! Let me sit down!
I can't find a place,* she says,
my mother
can't find a chair
to sit down on,
and when she's found one,
she tells me, *it's facing
the wrong direction!*

I can't tell her
it's 9 P.M. where I am,
and raining lightly.
I'm standing beside a fountain
in a slate-roofed town:

shutters
to keep my feelings out.

3. My Mother Yawns

Falls asleep with her
eyes open
and I wonder what
thoughts is she having there?

Sound
of nurses typing medical reports,
smells of coffee
and the humans
we were last discussing—

energy left in the air
the last thing my mom said: *they can
take a long time on purpose.*

Sometimes the whole poem
is the central image—

Sometimes
a smell, something
that happens only now.
Or is this an *always?*

4. Perfectly Fine

There's a man on her unit who
goes around shirtless.
A woman in white crocs comes
up and asks me *How old am I?*
Thirty-eight, I tell her.
You look about *thirty-eight.*

My mom appears well these
days— she smiles in selfies,
wears her leopard-print top
with sweatpants. When you meet
her, you might think she was
all smiles.

5. To See Clear

My mother lives
her life these days

as a poem with no images:
only sensory input

and gravitational waves
from far-off galaxies;

unquantifiable and
with no impact,

no touching, no
words like *skin*

for fear of accidentally
registering heat.

6. My Mother, The Rain

Summer rain is like my mother's eyes.
Its feeling is relief on a hot day.
The purpose of rain is to let nature
run its course. It rains
because it *has* to rain.

Her relatives are lakes,
fog, ice and snow.

Her complaint: not having
enough time to get
everything wet.

7. Teaching My Mother's Poetry Workshop

My mom would stamp people's
poems *Break My Heart*
when the poet
was holding something back.

I hold back something all the time:
my class-E felony in the
Commonwealth.

By now, I hope most people have
internalized this message—
so far, no one has brought a poem
that isn't at least chargeable
with Attempted Heartbreaking—

her demand was to
reveal absolutely *everything,*
leave nothing out
(in the first version).

8. July 19th

When cooking on a hot day,
she said to get the hot stuff done early—

my mom always made her gazpacho at the
first sign of a heat wave.

I could have given away her recipe,
the 1968 edition of *The Blender Cookbook,*
when I dismantled her apartment.

I memorized the recipe this time,
just in case.

Anyway there it is, my mom's gazpacho,
in my refrigerator right now, cooling.

9. Caregiver Fatigue

Heavy
has two meanings:
something that is massive (Sense 1)
something emotionally challenging (Sense 2).

When I handed Kathy my mom's financial
paperwork, she said *I hope you feel less
heavy now* (Sense 2: emotionally challenging).
Also, I gave up weightlifting (Sense 2:
emotionally challenging).

For me, there's a third kind of heavy:
like heavy rain.
It means relentless.

10. My Mom Categorizes Poems

- Good poem
- Bad poem (i.e. poems by Pinksy)
- Sonnet, haiku, etc.
- Sylvia Plath, Anne Sexton, anyone who killed herself
- Poems in which the poet is dead
- Frogsong misinterpreted as crickets
- Poetry suffering from travel-poem-itis
- Anything attributed to Shakespeare
- Online poems
- Any *send-it-to-The-New-Yorker*-style poem
- Screed
- *Break My Heart* poems
- *It's Cooked* poems
- Poems made during sex
- Poem found in bottle on remote beach
- Poems of madness (Baudelaire, Edgar Allan Poe, etc.)
- Poems my mom calls *genius*
- Poems by poets laureate other than Kay Ryan
- Poems my mom wrote, with me as a character
- Poems I write, with my mom as a character.

11. Eye Contact

Last week, when I visited
at the secure facility,
she was lost
in the corridor.
I walked her to her room,
stuck my face right in her face
and made eye contact.

My mother's eyes are blue these days.
She looks right at me, I see
the lights come on for an instant,
she says *I can't*
and lowers her head.

What is that *I can't?*
I obsess over its various possible
meanings: is she emotionally
incapable? Or should I take her
at her word she can't remember?
I try to read what I can
into her these days.

*These visits are so hard
for me,* she said today.
I know exactly
what she means.

ALZHEIMER'S FALL

1. The Wind Slams Eastward Down Beacon Street

It's Sabbath evening,
sundown 6:49 P.M
and I'm glad to have a psychic raincoat

that protects me from
harmful feelings, from
acid rain, from

her spirit in that place.
Mom, I told her last
time, *this is a holy place,*

like the image I have of my hometown
as *so tranquil.*
I pour a plastic cup

of Diet Ginger Ale for my mom,
pour a glass for me,
take a sip.

2. Janice

Janice,
my mother's childhood friend
came all the way from California
to see my mom,

who told Janice that she
and I had had a fight—

He got injured; I bled!

which we did in the sense
that my mom had dreamed
we'd had a fight—

my mom was shaken
by how real it seemed,

and afterward, Janice
collapsed, wounded, at my place,
in a deep panic
I'd never seen in her.

Next day, I call the hospital,
tell them *No more visitors*
for my mom.

She can't
sheathe her knives.

3. Razing The Tenements in Atlantic City

My mom asked the demolishers
if she could go inside
one last time
and we did— my brother,
our dad, our mom,
winter clouds—
it was my
first time in that building
though I knew every
hallway, every floorboard
of my mother's childhood.

In her bedroom, I stood
and looked at the ocean,
the crane with its yellow
wrecking ball.

My mom wrote this
poem already— her poem—
but I guess it's time for
me to write mine,

what that was like, I mean:
being her son,
standing in the wreckage.

4. On A Slippery Slope?

Take your grieving one spoonful
at a time, Srilatha tells me. *It will*
taste less bitter that way.

So I'm grieving my mother's
green cable-knit sweater—
I guess she'd knit it sometime
before I was born, because I
never saw her knit.

She always wore it when my brother
and I would come back from sledding
at the top of Summit Ave,
and there'd be hot chocolate,
and a fire in the fireplace—

my mom was always
great at fires, which surprises me
in retrospect: dirty stuff—

and my brother and I
would make dragons:
a roll of newspaper, folded over
and placed into the flames
would spew smoke from
its mouth, then burst—

is there any other word to use
than burst?

5. Unfilled Timetables

Things
bound for a destination
no one remembers.

The Yeats in me
wants to say *go back*
to the unfilled timetables

of April, the little bits
of spring that cling to her—
objects incoming

on waves, or clouds,
or the sky of whatever
moves her today.

6. June, 1982

It was 1982,
the summer my mom and I

took the bus to New York City
for the rally. *Don't have*

to pee, my mother warned me,
and I didn't.

It was an anti-nuclear rally
and the restroom attendant

at the Pierre Hotel
smiled and sprayed cologne

into the air
I walked through.

7. Take The 'Sim' Out of Simple

And replace it with a cat's purr
to make *purple.*

I think about what just
happened— the purple cat
I just created
stares at me.

I take the *purr*
from purple
replace it with cat pee
to make *people*

no more cat
just me
and my mom
and the way she
talks now:
I'm naked
as the day I was born!

8. The Dance Continued 'Til Two

I wanted to be
at the jam session
at the bar in St. John's—

but I was with my mom that night
eating Atlantic salmon in a pub
with a view of the ships
in St. John's Harbor.

I googled *cargo destinations Newfoundland,*
thinking it would be all about fishing—

I had been so romantic about
the stores of codfish I imagined
bound for North Carolina—

I believed life in Newfoundland
was all about fishing
but that's not been true for decades.

Search results: petroleum.
Russia. Iraq.

9. History Of Gunpowder

In this example, the history of
gunpowder is probably a metaphor
for my mom—
how dementia's made her forget
all her recipes, the poems she wrote,
everything dynamite
about her.

The gunpowder might also
not be a metaphor— if it
exploded, I mean, it would
be a real explosion, not
a riot of color or *an explosion
of feeling,* stuff
my mother used to say.

10. Because

That's why my notebooks
are full of dates— so I know when I

wrote what I wrote. I'm seeing
my life through the lens

of grief poems
about my mom, love poems

about Teddy and me,
and then the vast category

of *other* which is
either mysticism

or storytelling—
anything with stars in it.

11. Thanksgiving Day Is Hailed With Joy

It's November. Almost a year
since my mom had her episode—

a fall, a concussion,
a phone call from the E.R.—

Eric, I need you to come.
I was cooking dinner

for 10 at the time
and I sent a friend instead.

A year ago.
So many lasts of

the meantime— last time having
bagels in my mom's kitchen,

last time I searched her basement
for Viva paper towels.

12. Suppose We Could Do The Opposite

The inner light visible to no one.

The end-of-yoga-class light everyone
honors in each other.

The pale yellow sunlight
of the Sundays in my childhood
that proves I'm me.

The light in my apartment
on a Thursday
after everyone's had their fill;

the finished-poem light
that's gotten my poem to a place
where its needs are met.

Alzheimer's Winter

I. The Rest of The Coffee

Eric, I don't want to have Alzheimers,
my mom says.

I know, Mom. I wouldn't either.

All this, she says—

her upturned palm gestures
to the stopped grandfather
clock

to the murals on the wall
painted to look like
bookshelves full of books—

*You're responsible for all
of this,* as she takes my wrist.

Unfortunately, that's true, I tell her.

My mom says: *Well I hate it.*

I would hate it too.

2. Painted-On Contents of the Painted-On Bookshelves

There's Tolstoy in paperback.

They've got Emerson too,
Essays and Poems. Thoreau
must be painted on somewhere nearby.

A *New York Times Book of Houseplants*—
a quick glance around the unit reveals
two houseplants—
one in the Activity Room,
and yellow tea-roses
made of plastic.

This sylvan location
sheltered by snow-covered pines:
I feel we've reached
an alternate Walden.

3. From The Greek

I sort my problems these days
into two categories: solvable
problems, and aporias. Aporia
from the Greek word for *hole*
in the center of my universe:
a problem with no
solution.

In the realm of rhetoric,
aporia means *How can I even explain?*
or *What can I possibly do?*

Outside the realm of rhetoric
aporia (the philosophical kind)
includes things
like trauma—

because trauma has an
endless tail—

such as love,
the conditions
that make love impossible,

and grief
that can never be resolved.

4. I Don't Want To See This. I Don't.

She drinks four glasses
of cranberry juice
while I watch her worry
about the visit's end—

Eric, help me!
Stay more than a minute!
she begs me, her voice rising.

She grabs at my watch,
my orange plastic watch.
I take it off and put it
on her own wrist.
You know I'll never leave
without my watch, I say.

Later, when it really is
time for me to go, I
ask for my watch back.

It's our arrangement:
her permission.

5. Shiva

Wendy's brother has died
and I'm there on my mom's behalf:
because my mom
would know what to say,
and because, when my mom lost
her brother, no one cared enough.

Wendy's boss has sent round things:
a box of apples and oranges.

The fruit's still kosher
until the peel is removed:
can't trust the knives in someone
else's kitchen.

6. The Nutcracker

In one scene,
they wheeled in this
magical Christmas tree.
From our balcony seat
I could see the wires
holding up its massive top.

I was the sort of child who
could never suspend disbelief.
I named my animals descriptive names:
Brown Teddy. Blue Teddy.

I wouldn't call her lucid, exactly,
but yesterday when I showed her
the photo of Blue Teddy
she screamed *Blue Teddy!*

It's like that, our ballet:
the gestures
we both make.

7. Memories of Amsterdam

The tour of the Anne Frank House
is reduced to details:

the height-lines Anne and her siblings
penciled on the wall as they grew taller;

the gray smell
of that attic room,

and afterward, at the *Bloemenmarkt*
floating on the canal,

the way the tulips smelled
almost too real.

8. Now There's A Woman!

My mom has a phrase: *neat lady*
that she used to apply
to any woman she admired
yet somehow disliked.

If a woman was a lawyer,
she was almost automatically a
neat lady in my mom's book.

My mother almost went
to law school.
She got in, but didn't go.
And for much of my
childhood I wondered
what if she'd gone?

I'm pretty sure I wouldn't
exist in that scenario—
in that scenario,
she'd have married Tom Harris,
her college boyfriend,
who drove a motorcycle.

Like I said:
in that scenario,
I wouldn't exist.

9. Last Year

On the train ride home,
I can't stop thinking
about that stopped grandfather
clock in the lobby.
It's right twice a day.

Last year, I did battle
with the world
on my mom's behalf.

I'm the parent now,
I told the world.

Acknowledgements

For works previously published, I owe thanks to Margot Wizansky and Wendy Drexler, co-editors of "What The Poem Knows: A Tribute To Barbara Helfgott Hyett." My poem (now a chapter) "Alzheimer's Winter" was included in this beautiful Festschrift.

Thanks to Grey Held and Alexis Ivy for critiquing every poem in this book, crossing most things out, and generally making me a better poet.

Thanks to Heather Nelson and Spencer Thurlow for providing detailed feedback and bright ideas that led to the success of this endeavor.

Thanks to the members of the PoemWorks community, in Boston and around the world, for standing beside my mother and me throughout this ordeal.

Finally, my gratitude to all the members of the Friday Free Write group, where this book was composed in its entirety. Jonathan Aibel, Kirsten Alexander, Robert Carr, Sybil Byers Fetter, Johnny Gall, Kasha Martin Gauthier, Shana Hill, Linda Lamenza, Srilatha Rajamani, Kimberley Richardson, Maximilian Scherrer, Clara Silverstein, Kathy Whitham: thank you for sitting with me, listening to my words, and enabling me to tell this story.

Aporia is the debut collection of poetry by Eric E. Hyett. A poet and literary translator from Boston, Eric and his co-translator, Spencer Thurlow, made the shortlists for the 2018 National Translation Award and the 2018 Lucien Stryk Asian Translation Prize for their translation of *Sonic Peace* by contemporary Japanese female poet Minashita Kiriu (Phoneme Media, 2017). Eric's poems, essays and translations are part of the ongoing dialogue in *Granta, The Georgia Review, Lily Poetry Review, The Hudson Review, World Literature Today* and *Modern Poetry in Translation*. With *Aporia*, he seeks to engage the Alzheimer's community in meaningful conversation.

Photo: Kristina Watts

Aporia is the debut collection of poetry by Eric E. Hyett. A poet and literary translator from Boston, Eric and his co-translator, Spencer Thurlow, made the shortlists for the 2018 National Translation Award and the 2018 Lucien Stryk Asian Translation Prize for their translation of *Sonic Peace* by contemporary Japanese female poet Minashita Kiriu (Phoneme Media, 2017). Eric's poems, essays and translations are part of the ongoing dialogue in *Granta, The Georgia Review, Lily Poetry Review, The Hudson Review, World Literature Today* and *Modern Poetry in Translation.* With *Aporia*, he seeks to engage the Alzheimer's community in meaningful conversation.

CPSIA information can be obtained
at www.ICGtesting.com
Printed in the USA
BVHW080959110122
625980BV00005B/196